VICTORIA STATION
(From Other Places)

A Play

by Harold Pinter

‖SAMUEL FRENCH‖

samuelfrench.co.uk

Copyright © 1982 by Askerdale Limited
All Rights Reserved

VICTORIA STATION is fully protected under the copyright laws of the British Commonwealth, including Canada, the United States of America, and all other countries of the Copyright Union. All rights, including professional and amateur stage productions, recitation, lecturing, public reading, motion picture, radio broadcasting, television and the rights of translation into foreign languages are strictly reserved.

ISBN 978-0-573-04225-6

www.samuelfrench.co.uk
www.samuelfrench.com

For Amateur Production Enquiries

United Kingdom and World excluding North America

plays@samuelfrench.co.uk
020 7255 4302/01

Each title is subject to availability from Samuel French, depending upon country of performance.

CAUTION: Professional and amateur producers are hereby warned that *VICTORIA STATION* is subject to a licensing fee. Publication of this play does not imply availability for performance. Both amateurs and professionals considering a production are strongly advised to apply to the appropriate agent before starting rehearsals, advertising, or booking a theatre. A licensing fee must be paid whether the title is presented for charity or gain and whether or not admission is charged.

The professional rights in this play are controlled by Judy Daish Associates Ltd, 2 St Charles Pl, London W10 6EG.

No one shall make any changes in this title for the purpose of production. No part of this book may be reproduced, stored in a retrieval system, or transmitted in any form, by any means, now known or yet to be invented, including mechanical, electronic, photocopying, recording, videotaping, or otherwise, without the prior written permission of the publisher. No one shall upload this title, or part of this title, to any social media websites.

The right of Harold Pinter to be identified as author of this work has been asserted in accordance with Section 77 of the Copyright, Designs and Patents Act 1988.

THINKING ABOUT PERFORMING A SHOW?

There are thousands of plays and musicals available to perform from Samuel French right now, and applying for a licence is easier and more affordable than you might think

---

From classic plays to brand new musicals, from monologues to epic dramas, there are shows for everyone.

Plays and musicals are protected by copyright law, so if you want to perform them, the first thing you'll need is a licence. This simple process helps support the playwright by ensuring they get paid for their work and means that you'll have the documents you need to stage the show in public.

Not all our shows are available to perform all the time, so it's important to check and apply for a licence before you start rehearsals or commit to doing the show.

LEARN MORE & FIND THOUSANDS OF SHOWS

Browse our full range of plays and musicals, and find out more about how to license a show

www.samuelfrench.co.uk/perform

Talk to the friendly experts in our Licensing team for advice on choosing a show and help with licensing

plays@samuelfrench.co.uk   020 7387 9373

Acting Editions
BORN TO PERFORM

Playscripts designed from the ground up to work the way you do in rehearsal, performance and study

---

Larger, clearer text for easier reading

Wider margins for notes

Performance features such as character and props lists, sound and lighting cues, and more

---

+ CHOOSE A SIZE AND STYLE TO SUIT YOU

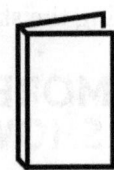 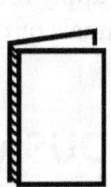 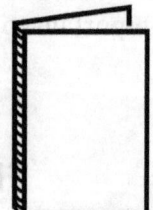

STANDARD EDITION — Our regular paperback book at our regular size

SPIRAL-BOUND EDITION — The same size as the Standard Edition, but with a sturdy, easy-to-fold, easy-to-hold spiral-bound spine

LARGE EDITION — A4 size and spiral bound, with larger text and a blank page for notes opposite every page of text – perfect for technical and directing use

LEARN MORE | samuelfrench.co.uk/actingeditions

**Other plays by HAROLD PINTER
published and licensed by Samuel French**

Celebration

The Birthday Party

The Caretaker

The Dumb Waiter

Family Voices (from the collection *Other Places*)

The Homecoming

A Kind of Alaska (from the collection *Other Places*)

The Lover

Mixed Doubles

Mountain Language

A Night Out

One for the Road (from the collection *Other Places*)

One to Another

The Room

A Slight Ache

**Other plays by HAROLD PINTER
licensed by Samuel French**

Apart from That

Ashes to Ashes

The Basement

Betrayal

The Black and White

The Dwarfs

The Hothouse

Landscape

Last To Go

Monologue

Moonlight

The New World Order

Night School

No Man's Land

Old Times

Party Time

Precisely

Press Conference

Request Stop

Silence

Tess

That's All

That's Your Trouble

Trouble in the Works

FIND PERFECT PLAYS TO PERFORM AT
www.samuelfrench.co.uk/perform

ABOUT THE AUTHOR

Harold Pinter was born in London in 1930. He lived with Antonia Fraser from 1975 until his death on Christmas Eve 2008. (They were married in 1980).

After studying at the Royal Academy of Dramatic Art and the Central School of Speech and Drama, he worked as an actor under the stage name David Baron. Following his success as a playwright, he continued to act under his own name, on stage and screen. He last acted in 2006 when he appeared in Beckett's *Krapp's Last Tape* at the Royal Court Theatre, directed by Ian Rickson.

He wrote twenty-nine plays including *The Birthday Party, The Dumb Waiter, A Slight Ache, The Hothouse, The Caretaker, The Collection, The Lover, The Homecoming, Old Times, No Man's Land, Betrayal, A Kind of Alaska, One For The Road, The New World Order, Moonlight* and *Ashes to Ashes*. Sketches include *The Black and White, Request Stop, That's your Trouble, Night, Precisely, Apart From that* and the recently rediscovered, *Umbrellas*.

He directed twenty-seven theatre productions, including James Joyce's *Exiles*, David Mamet's *Oleanna*, seven plays by Simon Gray (one of which was *Butley* in 1971 which he directed the film of three years later) and many of his own plays including his last, *Celebration*, paired with his first, *The Room* at The Almeida Theatre, London in the spring of 2000.

He wrote twenty-one screenplays including *The Pumpkin Eater, The Servant, The Go-Between, The French Lieutenant's Woman* and *Sleuth*.

In 2005 he received the Nobel Prize for Literature. Other awards include the Companion of Honour for services to Literature, the Legion D'Honneur, the European Theatre Prize the Laurence Olivier Award and the Moliere D'Honneur for lifetime achievement. In 1999 he was made a Companion of Literature by the Royal Society of Literature. Harold Pinter was awarded eighteen honorary degrees.

VICTORIA STATION

First performed as part of the quadruple bill *Other Places** in the Cottesloe auditorium of the National Theatre, London, on 14th October, 1982, with the following cast:

CONTROLLER   Paul Rogers
DRIVER   Martin Jarvis

Directed by Peter Hall
Designed by John Bury

* *Family Voices*, *A Kind of Alaska* and *One for the Road* are available separately in Acting Editions published by Samuel French.

To Mick Goldstein

The lights come up on an office. The **CONTROLLER** *is sitting at a microphone.*

CONTROLLER Two-seven-four? Where are you?

The lights come up on the **DRIVER** *in his car.*

Two-seven-four? Where are you?

Pause.

DRIVER Hullo?

CONTROLLER Two-seven-four?

DRIVER Hullo.

CONTROLLER Is that two-seven-four?

DRIVER That's me.

CONTROLLER Where are you?

DRIVER What?

Pause.

CONTROLLER I'm talking to two-seven-four? Right?

DRIVER Yes. That's me. I'm two-seven-four. Who are you?

Pause.

CONTROLLER Who am I?

DRIVER Yes.

CONTROLLER Who do you think I am? I'm your office.

DRIVER Oh yes.

CONTROLLER Where are you?

DRIVER I'm cruising.

CONTROLLER What do you mean?

Pause.

Listen, son. I've got a job for you. If you're in the area I think you're in. Where are you?

DRIVER I'm just cruising about.

CONTROLLER Don't cruise. Stop cruising. Nobody's asking you to cruise about. What the fuck are you cruising about for?

Pause.

Two-seven-four?

DRIVER Hullo. Yes. That's me.

CONTROLLER I want you to go to Victoria Station. I want you to pick up a customer coming from Boulogne. That is what I want you to do. Do you follow me? Now the question I want to ask you is this. Where are you? And don't say you're just cruising about. Just tell me if you're anywhere near Victoria Station.

DRIVER Victoria what?

Pause.

CONTROLLER Station.

Pause.

Can you help me on this?

DRIVER Sorry?

CONTROLLER Can you help me on this? Can you come to my aid on this?

Pause.

You see, two-seven-four, I've got no-one else in the area, you see. I've only got you in the area. I think. Do you follow me?

DRIVER I follow you, yes.

CONTROLLER And this is a good job, two-seven-four. He wants you to take him to Cuckfield.

DRIVER Eh?

CONTROLLER He wants you to take him to Cuckfield. You're meeting the ten twenty-two from Boulogne. The European Special. His name's MacRooney. He's a little bloke with a limp. I've known him for years. You pick him up under the clock. You'll know him by his hat. He'll have a hat on with a feather in it. He'll be carrying fishing tackle, two-seven-four?

DRIVER Hullo?

CONTROLLER Are you hearing me?

DRIVER Yes.

Pause.

CONTROLLER What are you doing?

DRIVER I'm not doing anything.

CONTROLLER How's your motor? Is your motor working?

DRIVER Oh yes.

CONTROLLER Your ignition's not on the blink?

DRIVER No.

CONTROLLER So you're sitting in a capable car?

DRIVER I'm sitting in it, yes.

CONTROLLER Are you in the driving seat?

Pause.

Do you understand what I mean?

Pause.

Do you have a driving wheel in front of you?

Pause.

Because I haven't, two-seven-four. I'm just talking into this machine, trying to make some sense out of our lives. That's my function. God gave me this job. He asked me to do this job, personally. I'm your local monk, two-seven-four. I'm a monk. You follow? I lead a restricted life. I haven't got a choke and a gear lever in front of me. I haven't got a cooling system and four wheels. I'm not sitting here with wing mirrors and a jack in the boot. And if I did have a jack in the boot I'd stick it right up your arse.

Pause.

Listen, two-seven-four. I've got every reason to believe that you're driving a Ford Cortina, I would very much like you to go to Victoria Station. *In* it. That means I don't want you to walk down there. I want you to drive down there. Right?

DRIVER Everything you say is correct. This is a Ford Cortina.

CONTROLLER Good. That's right. And you're sitting in it while we're having this conversation, aren't you?

DRIVER That's right.

CONTROLLER Where?

DRIVER By the side of a park.

CONTROLLER By the side of a park?

DRIVER Yes.

CONTROLLER What park?

DRIVER A dark park.

CONTROLLER Why is it dark?

Pause.

DRIVER That's not an easy question.

Pause.

CONTROLLER Isn't it?

DRIVER No.

Pause.

CONTROLLER You remember this customer I was talking to you about? The one who's coming in to Victoria Station? Well, he's very keen for you to take him down to Cuckfield. He's got an old aunt down there. I've got a funny feeling she's going to leave him all her plunder. He's going down to pay his respects. He'll be in a good mood. If you play your cards right you might come out in front. Get me?

Pause.

Two-seven-four?

DRIVER Yes? I'm here.

CONTROLLER Go to Victoria Station.

DRIVER I don't know it.

CONTROLLER You don't know it?

DRIVER No. What is it?

Silence.

CONTROLLER It's a station, two-seven-four.

Pause.

Haven't you heard of it?

DRIVER No. Never. What kind of place is it?

Pause.

CONTROLLER You've never heard of Victoria Station?

DRIVER Never. No.

CONTROLLER It's a famous station.

DRIVER Well, I honestly don't know what I've been doing all these years.

CONTROLLER What have you been doing all these years?

DRIVER Well, I honestly don't know.

Pause.

CONTROLLER All right, two-seven-four. Report to the office in the morning. One-three-five? Where are you? One-three-five? Where are you?

DRIVER Don't leave me.

CONTROLLER What? Who's that?

DRIVER It's me. Two-seven-four. Please. Don't leave me.

CONTROLLER One-three-five? Where are you?

DRIVER Don't have anything to do with one-three-five. He's not your man. He'll lead you into blind alleys by the dozen. They all will. Don't leave me. I'm your man. I'm the only one you can trust.

Pause.

CONTROLLER Do I know you, two-seven-four? Have we met?

Pause.

Well, it'll be nice to meet you in the morning. I'm really looking forward to it. I'll be sitting here with my cat o'nine tails, son. And you know what I'm going to do with it? I'm going to tie you up bollock naked to a butcher's table and I'm going to flog you to death all the way to Crystal Palace.

DRIVER That's where I am! I knew I knew the place.

Pause.

I'm sitting by a little dark park underneath Crystal Palace. I can see the Palace. It's silhouetted against the sky. It's a wonderful edifice, isn't it?

Pause.

My wife's in bed. Probably asleep. And I've got a little daughter.

CONTROLLER Oh, you've got a little daughter?

Pause.

DRIVER Yes, I think that's what she is.

CONTROLLER Report to the office at nine a.m. One-three-five? Where are you? Where the fuck is one-three-five? Two-four-six? One-seven-eight? One-o-one? Will somebody help me? Where's everyone gone? I've got a good job going down to Cuckfield. Can anyone hear me?

DRIVER I can hear you.

CONTROLLER Who's that?

DRIVER Two-seven-four. Here. Waiting. What do you want me to do?

CONTROLLER You want to know what I want you to do?

DRIVER Oh by the way, there's something I forgot to tell you.

CONTROLLER What is it?

DRIVER I've got a P.O.B.

CONTROLLER You've got a P.O.B.?

DRIVER Yes. That means passenger on board.

CONTROLLER I know what it means, two-seven-four. It means you've got a passenger on board.

DRIVER That's right.

CONTROLLER You've got a passenger on board sitting by the side of a park?

DRIVER That's right.

CONTROLLER Did I book this job?

DRIVER No, I don't think you came into it.

CONTROLLER Well, where does he want to go?

DRIVER He doesn't want to go anywhere. We just cruised about for a bit and then we came to rest.

CONTROLLER In Crystal Palace?

DRIVER Not *in* the Palace.

CONTROLLER Oh, you're not *in* the Palace?

DRIVER No. I'm not right inside it.

CONTROLLER I think you'll find the Crystal Palace burnt down years ago, old son. It burnt down in the Great Fire of London.

Pause.

DRIVER Did it?

CONTROLLER Two-seven-four?

DRIVER Yes. I'm here.

CONTROLLER Drop your passenger. Drop your passenger at his chosen destination and proceed to Victoria Station. Otherwise I'll destroy you bone by bone. I'll suck you in and blow you out in little bubbles. I'll chew your stomach out with my own teeth. I'll eat all the hair off your body. You'll end up looking like a pipe cleaner. Get me?

Pause.

Two-seven-four?

Pause.

You're beginning to obsess me. I think I'm going to die. I'm alone in this miserable freezing fucking office and nobody loves me. Listen, pukeface—

DRIVER Yes?

Pause.

CONTROLLER One-three-five? One-three-five? Where are you?

DRIVER Don't have anything to do with one-three-five. They're all blood-suckers. I'm the only one you can trust.

Pause.

CONTROLLER You know what I've always dreamed of doing? I've always had this dream of having a holiday in sunny Barbados. I'm thinking of taking this holiday at the end of this year, two-seven-four. I'd like you to come with me. To Barbados. Just the two of us. I'll take you snorkelling. We can swim together in the blue Caribbean.

Pause.

In the meantime, though, why don't you just pop back to the office now and I'll make you a nice cup of tea? You can tell me something about your background, about your ambitions and aspirations. You can tell me all about your little hobbies and pastimes. Come over and have a nice cup of tea, two-seven-four.

DRIVER I'd love to but I've got a passenger on board.

CONTROLLER Put your passenger on to me. Let me have a word with him.

DRIVER I can't. She's asleep on the back seat.

CONTROLLER She?

DRIVER Can I tell you a secret?

CONTROLLER Please do.

DRIVER I think I've fallen in love. For the first time in my life.

CONTROLLER Who have you fallen in love with?

DRIVER With this girl on the back seat. I think I'm going to keep her for the rest of my life. I'm going to stay in this car with her for the rest of my life. I'm going to marry her in this car. We'll die together in this car.

Pause.

CONTROLLER So you've found true love at last, eh, two-seven-four?

DRIVER Yes. I've found true love at last.

CONTROLLER So you're a happy man now then, are you?

DRIVER I'm very happy. I've never known such happiness.

CONTROLLER Well, I'd like to be the first to congratulate you, two-seven-four. I'd like to extend my sincere felicitations to you.

DRIVER Thank you very much.

CONTROLLER Don't mention it. I'll have to make a note in my diary not to forget your Golden Wedding, won't I? I'll bring along some of the boys to drink your health. Yes, I'll bring along some of the boys. We'll all have a few jars and a bit of a sing-song.

Pause.

Two-seven-four?

Pause.

DRIVER Hullo. Yes. It's me.

CONTROLLER Listen. I've been thinking. I've decided that what I'd like to do now is to come down there and shake you by the hand straightaway. I'm going to shut this little office and I'm going to jump into my old car and I'm going to pop down to see you, to shake you by the hand. All right?

DRIVER Fine. But what about the man coming off the train at Victoria Station—the ten twenty-two from Boulogne?

CONTROLLER He can go and fuck himself.

DRIVER I see.

CONTROLLER No, I'd like to meet your lady friend, you see. And we can have a nice celebration. Can't we? So just stay where you are. Right?

Pause.

Right?

Pause.

Two-seven-four?

DRIVER Yes?

CONTROLLER Don't move. Stay exactly where you are. I'll be right with you.

DRIVER No, I won't move.

Silence.

I'll be here.

The lights go out in the office. The **DRIVER** *sits still. The lights go out in the car.*

Curtain.

FURNITURE AND PROPERTY LIST

Onstage: OFFICE
               Desk. *On it:* microphone
               Chair

               CAR
               Driver's seat
               Hand radio mouthpiece

Offstage: Nil

LIGHTING PLOT

Property fittings required: nil

To open: Lighting up on office area

Cue 1	**Controller:** "Two-seven-four? Where are you?" *Lighting up on car area*	(Page 1)
Cue 2	**Driver:** "I'll be here." *Fade office area lighting*	(Page 11)
Cue 3	**Driver** sits still *Fade car area lighting*	(Page 11)

EFFECTS PLOT

No cues

VISIT THE SAMUEL FRENCH BOOKSHOP AT THE ROYAL COURT THEATRE

Browse plays and theatre books, get expert advice and enjoy a coffee

Samuel French Bookshop
Royal Court Theatre
Sloane Square
London
SW1W 8AS
020 7565 5024

Shop from thousands of titles on our website

 samuelfrench.co.uk

 samuelfrenchltd

 samuel french uk

www.ingramcontent.com/pod-product-compliance
Lightning Source LLC
Chambersburg PA
CBHW070456050426
42450CB00012B/3300